Y0-DOI-503

"love bears all things, believes all things, hopes all things, endures all things. Love never ends"

1 Corinthians 13:7, 8

© 2023 by Nancy Grandquist

All rights reserved. This book or any portion thereof may not be reproduced or used in any manner whatsoever without the express written permission of the publisher except for the use of brief quotations in a book review.

Printed in the United States of America
First Printing, 2023
ISBN 978-1-7331248-8-1

Purpose Media Publishing
P.O. Box 15561
Little Rock, AR 72231
For information on ordering this book and others,
visit Purposemediapublishing.com/MySpecialsomeone

purposemediapublishing.com

Dedication

This book is a love letter with beautifully hand-drawn portraits that will speak to every heart from the youngest child to the oldest of all. I dedicate this book to my late brother David who was the pied piper to his children and all of mine too. I miss him more with every passing year.

*Special thanks to my niece Nora Jean, my brother David's baby girl, for bringing my words on the pages of this book to life with every stroke of your brush. I love you.

Aunt Nan

My special one

You're like the snickering,
silly smile of the madman
in the moon

You're like the silky satin
stocking made from a worm's
cozy cocoon

You're like the sky
homemade in Montana right
out of the big blue

And you, you are my
special one

You're like a puff of cream
piled high on top of my
favorite dream

You're like a fudge bar bite
at midnight; do you know
what I mean?

You're like a holly
and a berry that's
sure to be merry at a
Christmas sing

And you, you are my
special one.

You're like a vintage,
priceless piece of all my
treasured memories

You're like a seedling planted
deep that's sprouting joyful,
peaceful things

You're like a perfect rainbow's
end—a pot of gold, that's you—
but much more than just a friend

You, you are my
special one

You're like a hairless,
toothless baby that steals
my grouch away

You're like Duck, Duck,
and Monopoly; you teach
me how to play

You're like a word and
a faithful promise that
everything will be okay

and you, you are my
special one

My Special One, My Special One

You are an icon;
you are eclectic;
you are sweet,
good, and fun

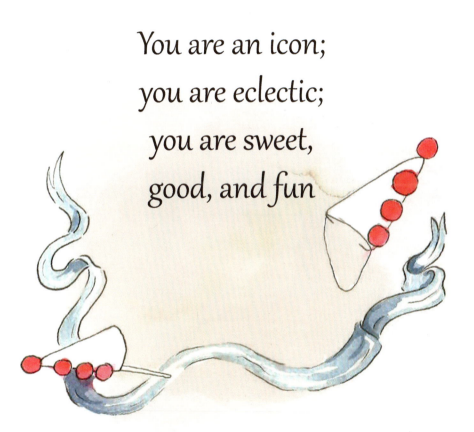

My special one, my special one

I love you better and need you
more than the stars, the moon,
and the morning sun

My special one

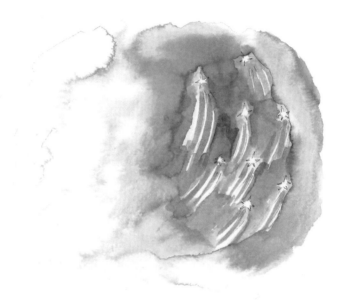

The End